I Wrote A Poem For You

Sasha Nudél

I Wrote A Poem For You

www.sashanudel.com

ISBN: 979-8-218-29292-8
Illustrations by: Anfisa Kuzmina
Edited by: Jordyn Denning

Dedicated to all the incurable romantics…

Also by Sasha Nudél
A Mouth Full Of Lust

LOVE, ALWAYS

Home

My home is not in an opulent entrance,
sophisticated crown moldings or grand staircase.
My home is not in a flawlessly made up bed.
It's in the way your chest is carved perfectly to
cushion my head.
My home is not in expensive dishes.
It's in the way you unravel my **inhibitions**.
My home is not in a prestigious address.
It's in the way you can't help but slip your hand
under my dress.
My home is not in designer baggage.
It's in our inside jokes and secret language.
My home is not in **ceaselessly** sunny weather.
It's in the way we are never not laughing together.
My home is not in the custom-made window
panes.
It's in the silliness of our pet names.
My home is not in a list of guests too long to
remember.
It's in how desperate we are for each other's
forever.

Me Before You

Absentmindedly wandering
down memory lane
in search of Me Before You,
but to no avail.

Jaded

Can we linger in the infatuation phase a little
longer?
Before time brings our flaws to light.
Before we regret our confessions.
Before the threads that bind us together begin to
fray.
Before I become jaded and you, heartbroken.
Hurry.
Pour yourself onto me like honey.
Against better judgment.
Mold into the crevices of my soul.
A meaningful bond, albeit short-lived.
And please, do that thing I love the most,
where you grip my throat like a vice and kiss it.
Hurry. Before the sun burns itself out.

Scent

Your fantasies will forever carry my scent.

12

Worth It

I want to spend my love on you,
but these sparks are burning my lungs.
In this battle of tongues,
smiles against mouths,
vows against hours,
my gloss staining your lips,
your stubbornness drowns,
and all you hear is unrestrained,
insatiable vowels.
True love always requires poor timing.
'Madness' tattooed over your heart.
My failed rhyming.
This love story is written into cement.
I am lovesick.
I am love-spent.
This heartache is coursing through my aorta,
but the havoc our farewell wreaked on my being
was worth it.

Since The Day

A persistent sunray is playing peeping Tom
through my curtains, hoping to witness what the
Universe has been gossiping about since the day
our lips touched.

Missing From Me

It's not that I miss you.
It's that you are missing from me.
In that sunken area between the heart and the
breastbone,
where the emptiness stabs into flesh
more harshly than the pointed end of a broken
bone.
Oh why am I not made of stone!
This rupture is oozing.
And to remedy the sharp pain, the swelling and
bruising,
I keep looking for you
in the 366th day of the year,
eighth day of the week,
25th hour,
61st second.
All in vain.
Perhaps, I lost you in the fifth season.
Will you tell me the reason?

Not Enough

Forever falls short of the time I need with you.

16

Wild Abandon

Touch me in earnest.
Purposeful and meticulous
strokes of grandeur
along my sternum.
Feel every thrum of my pulse,
every beat of my heart.
Stay there, frozen in my words,
heated in my stare.
Plunge headlong into the pools of my collarbones.
Immerse yourself in my being, deep,
breath held, feelings exacerbated,
for I am yours to make you feel
with wild abandon.

Unlike Any

I put my hand on your chest and hear your inner world tap-dancing in perfect rhythm with my heartbeat. A certain euphoria creeps into my awareness along with the feeling of absolute emotional clarity unlike any I had ever known. I am in love.

My First

You were my first.
No, not the kiss.
You were my first lost-in-the-moment bliss.
No, not my first crush.
But the swirl of your tongue was the cause
for this everlasting adrenaline rush.
No, not the first to throb at the sight of my
curves.
You were the first to give pulse to my words.
No, not my first fantasy.
But the reason I've experienced ecstasy.
No, not my first love.
But when my heart smiles,
you are the only one I can think of

Camera Roll

I wish I could download our memories into my camera roll for some hard evidence of our evanescent story.

Used For Art

I'm afraid I brought you here
under false pretenses,
but since you awakened my senses,
       I figured using you for my art
      is a pure intention.
       So come here,
          drop all your defenses.
         Can you feel my
         heat
         seeping into your
         flesh?
           Breathe me
           in.
        Love me
        senseless.
        Maybe later,
        we'll worry about
        the consequences.

Self-care

You are my self-care and I would like to practice
you with reckless abandon.

Sensible Love

Is there a sensible way to love?
A way to calculate and weigh up
all cons and pros,
to predict and avoid any loss,
to chart love's trajectory
and approach your decision objectively?
The problem is,
there isn't a scale to weigh the giddy release in my
tummy,
his encyclopedic knowledge of my body,
the effortless conversation shared between two,
the laughter leaving my ribs sore.
Even the post-breakup agony.
Yes, it hurts, but please give me more.
The answer is 'no.'
Sensible love is an oxymoron.
I want it to feel counterintuitive. Different.
Foreign.
I want no part of my soul left untouched,
each mouth's corner left upturned.
The only sensible way to love
is the one where you're willing and eager to get
burned.

Affected

You tell me my skin feels like satin,
but can you feel how affected
it is by the art of your tactics
during our frequent practice?
As if the earth spins off its axis.

Phenomenon

My rational thoughts have disappeared under
mysterious circumstances,
similar to the strange phenomena observed in the
Bermuda Triangle.
The geometry of your shoulders, your tongue's
gentle swirl,
hauled me into this hazardous place, this realm of
no return.
And it wouldn't be a concern
had the rest of the world not completely lost me
to you.
Had you not had the need to wreck another ship.
Had you not had the need to collect a new trinket
while this one's still sinking.
Gasping for air.
How do I swim out of this abyss?
How do I, after my draining endeavor to try to
rise above nature,
forsaken the lover-turned-stranger
in order to set myself free?
Instead, I keep aching over you being a thousand
kisses away from me.

Gravitational

'Your words are honey,' he says with an
unwavering gaze.
His voice resonates through my chest wall and
spreads across my skin.
I smile my thanks and scribble 'gravitational' on
my wrist.

Bright Eyes

In the impatience of bated breath.
In the vibrancy of rosy lips.
In his lightness and great depth.
In the significance of his fingertips.
In the playfulness of his voice.
In the urgency to make plans.
In his carefree nature of choice
and the mightiness of his hands.
Under the curtains of my own eyelashes.
In the stare of his bright eyes.
In the deepening of all six senses
is where my desire lies.

Us

His soft soul and rough hands.
My soft hands and rough soul.

Perfect Rhyme

There go her demons so masterfully disguised in
the grin,
on her skin,
and the essence within
seducing me once more.
You would think that shiver down in my core
and the sirens going off in my veins
would remind of the pain,
of the time she has split my life in
'unremarkable' and 'amused to have finally found
a muse.'
But when her wild has enveloped my mind
and grown roots around my spine,
I realized that she and I are a perfect rhyme.

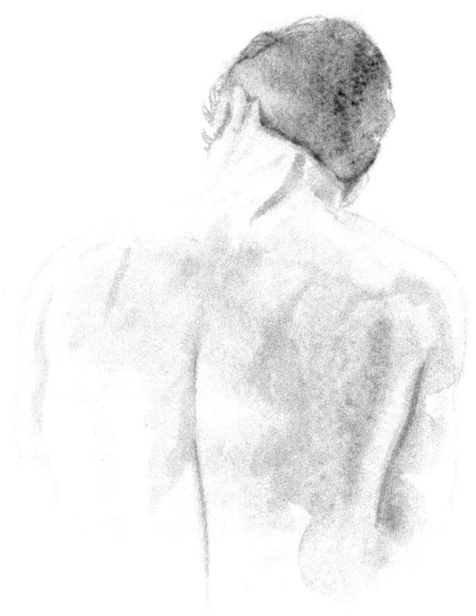

The Worst Thing

Let's just go for it! What is the worst thing that can happen? You are going to turn me into a memory and I am going to turn you into poetry. And in both spaces we live on infinitely.

Spring

I am Winter.
I am cold, often bad-tempered,
unnecessarily harsh but secretly gentle.
Whereas she is Spring.
By nature, she can melt heavy snowdrifts
that veil a numb heart.
And her lyrical touch lulls my heart
into the most peaceful daydream imaginable,
where I can foresee the inevitable:
a delicate flower grows roots inside a rock.
And paper beats rock for a reason.
With each passing season,
 she sprouts more flowers around my collarbones.
Now I am never alone.
She is proof
that open heart prevails over aloof,
sensitive over ruthless,
warm over cold,
because softness is bold.
Softness is Spring,
and my Spring gives me wings.

Look Up

I scribbled my poems into the clouds so that you could read my mind every time you look up at the sky.

Look Up

I scribbled my poems into the clouds so that you could read my mind every time you look up at the sky.

Tragic

The burning question is,
after all the 'almosts' hiding
in smoldering looks,
fingertip games,
the corner-of-the-mouth kiss magic,
how passionate can love possibly be
if it's not at least a little bit tragic?

Extraordinary

And I will always remember you for the way your
vibrant touch rebelled against my dull routine and
turned ordinary into extra. For the way your
fingers would summon goosebumps upon my skin
and kisses give rise to a cathartic release, or what I
like to call, poetry.

Consumed Alive

I am an all-in kind of hopeless romantic,
for diluted love tastes like lukewarm cocoa to me.
I would rather burn my whole mouth on the most
flavorful feeling,
have it melt deeply into me and consume me alive,
than dip my tongue into something unremarkable.

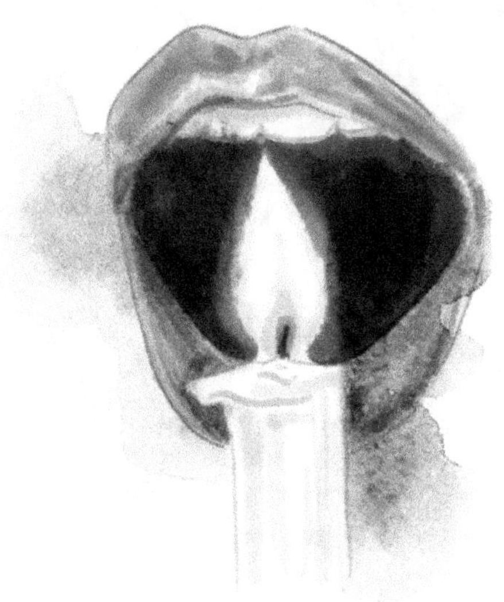

Submission

I let my ego submit to your love,
my logic to your lightheartedness,
my pride to your vulnerability.
All after you made my guard submit to your
hands.

Protect

He said,
"I'll protect you from all of your vividly painful
dreams,
and when I hear your soul scream,
I'll keep it gently cradled
to protect you from egos overinflated.
When empty words are thrown your way
causing you pain,
I'll be your Novocaine."
He said,
"I'll protect you from mannequin souls,
from villains and trolls,
from the remnants of your emotional past.
I'll even protect you from time flying too fast.
For insecurities and all the vices,
I'll remind you that perfection is lifeless."
He concluded,
"To the love of my life,
while simultaneously found and lost,
I'm afraid
I need to protect you from me the most."

Right Back In

Unsubscribe.
Unfollow.
Unfriend.
Deactivate.
Delete.
Disappear.
Detox.
Lock eyes.
Fall right back in.

Love Or Lust?

Tender is the way to handle
this delicate treasure
whose delicious lingering flavor
turned my bleakness to pleasure,
whose fine aftertaste can't be erased.
Her.
The one who aroused
an incandescent yearning for more.
The one who made me question reality under my
feet and up above.
How do I know if what I feel is
scorching lust or counterintuitive love?

Panacea

Your mighty hands coalesce so seamlessly with my delicate skin. I can sense the panacea for my happiness on the tips of your fingers.

Cupid's Error

No one is entirely immune to Cupid's arrow.
The self-proclaimed ice queen has been finally
struck,
he did not spare her.
It is the end of an era.
Vulnerability no longer gives rise to terror.
The igloo her heart calls a home melts,
breaths finally change to deep from shallow.
However,
just temporarily. Not forever.
Despite it being a sincere endeavor,
an empath fell in love with a narcissist,
and down her cheeks goes her mascara.
Turns out, Cupid's arrow was shot in a terrible
error.

Nice Seeing You

Saw you earlier today at the corner of my
unconscious and wakefulness. You looked sleepy
and so kissable, but I didn't have the heart to
approach you.
Hope all is well.

In My Arms

My bed has swallowed our antics.
This connection is hard to explain.
Cynics always lose to romantics,
hence the need to kiss her again.

I can feel her pulse in my temples.
I must be going insane.
With her, life art resembles.
Without, an indescribable pain.

Egos are burning bridges,
whirlwinds derail the trains.
Doors spin off their hinges,
but she's in my arms again.

In Love

In chaos we met.
In madness we grew.
In heartache we yearned.
In solitude we realized.
In uncertainty we leapt.
In love we fell.

"I Love You"

I have a beautiful memory of the time
when the 'I' in the most coveted 3-word phrase
spoken by you sounded convincing.
And in no way am I dismissing
the effort you've put into the striking
performance.
Bravo!
Your acting was flawless,
the impact – enormous,
but I will not be shouting 'Encore.'

Ego

Overcast
over my heart
over a boy
whose ego tore us apart.

Reckless

Like the sky needing a star.
Like water satisfying severe thirst.
If I get her back, the Universe loves me.
If she's just a dream, I've been cursed.

It's our bodies' alchemical cadence.
It's the way her heart relaxes my clenched fists.
I am willing to learn patience
just to kiss her delicate wrists.

She detonates stars behind my lids,
unveiling our undeniable
gravitational pull.
Her softness changes the
course of strong winds.
Here I am, reckless in
love, charging at red
bull.

One Fear

Them: What was it about her that made you want
to do better?
Him: It was the way she looked at me as if a
coward like me could do no wrong. She fed me
courage and starved me of my fears.
All but one.
The fear of losing her.

Wishful Apology

Hey you. Yes, you, my midnight madness.
My morning ache. My daily sadness.
Although a hundred lies too late I am,
I'll try with everything I can
to show the deep regret I now exist with,
the nagging scar inside my soul.
And I'd give everything I own
to reincarnate you in my arms.
I'm sorry to have caused you harm.
Now until the very end of time,
to alleviate this pain of mine,
all I can do is punch walls, throw fists and scream
over the pain I've put you through,
and for destroying my own dream
of dancing for eons upon this earth with you.

No More

Somewhere between 'meant to be' and 'we are
no more.'
Somewhat blessed and doomed at the same time.
Sort of at peace but also kind of at war,
now that I'm still yours, but you are no longer
mine.

Wild Animals

Having touched you once,
the wild animals
inside my cells
released chemicals,
and they rebelled
against the skepticism
that's overtaken my heart.
My love,
I tamed those wild animals,
and those excruciating memories
are now my worst enemies,
for they are haunting my reveries
while you and I are apart.
I'll fight for you for months, years, and centuries.
Your arms, your eyes, your lips are my remedies
against the trivial pleasantries.
You're all the beautiful melodies,
and one of life's biggest tragedies is
that mine you are not.

Revolutionary

They had this potent connection, the kind of magic no one could understand in this rational, practical and predictable world. A spiritual mystery between two brave souls that had thrown every single one of their doubts and fears into uproar. Can you just picture two people needing to ration their breathing at the sight of each other? Two souls simultaneously being each other's agony and solace. Is it even real love if it's not revolutionary?

Masterpiece

I once stumbled upon a striking piece of art. His grandiosity could feel intimidating - a handsome glass mosaic inlaid with small colored fragments of his past and present seducing my senses. True to its definition, the art piece invoked a reaction by disrupting my inner peace. Awakened and intrigued, I looked closer. I studied him. Every crack, scratch, and all the plaster holding his pieces together. Blinded by infatuation for the masterpiece, I let him consume me, until one day I looked too close and saw right through him. The newly discovered truths exploded in a mass of fiery shards and bit into my chest. Pain ripped through me so fast, it took my heart rate from steady to wild in a beat. In that clarifying moment, I realized that art is not meant to be intellectualized, but rather reveled in.

Unmatched

His perception
of my body's reaction
and its warm reception
to his affection
is uncanny.
His attention to detail
unmatched,
and the reason I've been coveting his touch
since the moment we got detached.

Her

"Mind if I use you to enrich my writing life?
You don't have to do anything but exist."
It's like testing the blade of a carving knife,
when thoughts of her I try to resist.
Thoughts, dreams, rhymes so revealing
when two souls are completely entwined.
When I'm asked to describe the most satisfying
feeling,
only her name comes to mind.

Less Thinking

I haven't the faintest idea how to collect my
thoughts after you punctuate my ramblings with a
kiss. 'Less thinking, more kissing' it is.

Every Lifetime

I am convinced
we have touched each other
in every lifetime.
It must be the way
my body trembles in recognition,
hands stutter in their motion,
and the sound of my heartbeat
reverberates on every frequency
that proves me right.

His Hands

My eyelids get heavy with visions of us swirling through my head, where his hands, having a natural bent for throwing my body over its sensitivity threshold, instigate goosebumps across my skin yet again. His effort, might and mischievous smile all play havoc with my discipline. We find our carefree joy in the aftertaste of each other, and in full surrender, we decide that space is not welcome between us.

Velvet

I still remember the smell of her velvet skin,
and not to worship it
would be a sin.
Her mischievous grin
would drive a crazy man crazier.
That damn velvet skin.
I still remember the warmth of her fingertips.
The only thing softer and warmer
were her lips.
Without them, my soul is in a total lunar eclipse.
The kind that makes a dark headspace darker.
Those damn fingertips.
I still remember that feeling of carefree.
How lightweight she was when it came to wine
and me.
How knowing that
would make me break out in a fever of glee.
The kind that makes a happy man happier.
That damn feeling of carefree.
I still remember the sound of her laughter,
and how nothing but making her smile mattered.
It was that sweet giggle I was after.
The kind that makes a weak man feel like the
mightiest.
That damn sound of laughter.
I don't remember my life before her.
There was nothingness and then my desperate
need to conquer.
Did I get scared? What possessed me to wrong
her?
Explosion then, poof. She is mine no longer.

Spoken Language

They spoke a language
of passionate exaggeration,
enunciating every thought,
touch,
feeling,
leaving no space for misinterpretation.

Jugular

Nature roars, ground shakes.
Here comes my internal earthquake.
Love throbs dangerously in my jugular vein.
Are you my safe haven or life-threatening pain?
The gentle vulgarity of our touch,
and there is no such thing as too much,
when in one destined motion
two rivers flow into one ocean.

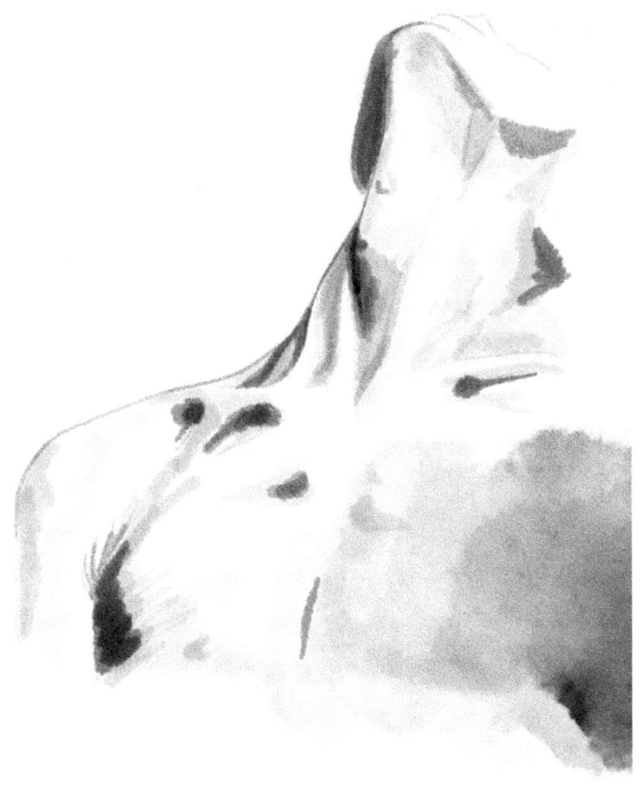

Threat

A sip of my jasmine tea
while overindulging in chocolate
topped with an edible flower.
The smell of your neck,
and like anything else
that's this sweet,
you are a threat to my willpower.

Bigger Than Us

It was bigger than us.
The kind of uncompromisingly passionate
togetherness
that scared us.
We kissed abundantly,
touched worshipfully,
fucked radically,
loved artfully.
It was bigger than us.
It was.

Leaver

Went in for a kiss
and tripped on his ego.
That is one way
to turn a lover into a leaver.

Soar

With my breath caught in my throat,
am I drowning or staying afloat?
The unconscious thoughts seep into the
conversation
at the least provocation.
We tease each other's willpower.
You insist, "One cannot be a hero without first
being a coward."
I overcome all my fears completely,
and your warmth melts into me deeply.
Reality blends into fantasy and vice versa.
Our vital organs are bursting.
A raging inferno has overtaken my core.
You're teaching me that I don't need planes to
soar.

Can You Feel

Can you feel my heart waves in your brainwaves?
Have my high-octane desires succeeded in
connecting to you energetically?

Heart Overuse

Last night I lived a morbid dream.
I was awakened by a scream,
distinctly sounding like a wounded soul
losing all of her control.
Last night I visited a graveyard of words unsaid,
and caught off guard
to have found a plot
to lay my heart to rest half dead.
And in my dream state,
immobilized,
I analyzed the heart and realized
the pain he caused metastasized.
How do I shake myself awake?
What caused my heart to break?
He cost me all I had to lose.
My heart expired due to overuse.
How do I forget all this?
I think now it's only fair for me to bury his.

Coward

We got separated by a drawbridge.
I needed you to jump and close the gap between
us,
but you didn't take that leap.

Victory

Here I am
in this blanket fort, falling victim
to your proprietorial mouth.
And as our battle of tongues
goes down in history,
a triumphal arch spans my lower back,
commemorating your victory.

Feverish

Am I falling victim to sunstroke, or is it just your
kisses working me into a blissful fever?

Couldn't Fool

I couldn't fool you
with my coy smile and quiet demeanor,
for when you kissed me
my eyes told all my feelings,
my skin spilled all my secrets,
and my heart burst at the seams.

My Delight

As I relish the weight of your body
in the flush of the morning light,
the sun's painting my cheeks scarlet,
and in the crook of your neck
I find my delight.

White Flag

He went to war against my **fears,**
annihilating them with his love.
I might've raised the white flag
in surrender and submission,
but by no means was it defeat.

Open

You made my frown lines soften.
You made my laugh lines deepen.
You broke my rib cage open
to let your love seep in.

Mountainous

On top of you
I am rising and falling.
Up that bulging neck vein
my fingers are crawling.
The sculpted lines of your shoulders
giving rise to these mountainous feelings
and together we're soaring.

Survival

This pleasure is so filling,
it clogs my veins,
my heart skips beats,
yet I feel so alive.
This pleasure
burns through
my bloodstream
and your mouth-to-mouth
is what I need to survive.

Love Multiplies

I am musing on a mental photograph I took
of our ravenous last night.
It's hard to sum everything meaningful
in a sound bite,
so I put pen to paper,
postpone life to later.
Relive those moments through cursive
and despite being nervous,
I dedicate to you these verses.
Bed, hair, and thoughts disheveled.
Connection to real life severed.
We're blossoming in each other's arms,
my hands pressed on the wall by your palms.
You're outlining a heart on my cheek with the
tip of your nose.
Your feelings exposed.
And in this life of
uncertainty,
with this feeling
of urgency,
in this moment,
right this second,
we can see in
each other's
eyes
how our love
multiplies.

Turbulent

The smooth sailing of his thumb
across my bottom lip
washed away all of my reservations.
And all of a sudden, I wanted him
to make my calm waters turbulent.

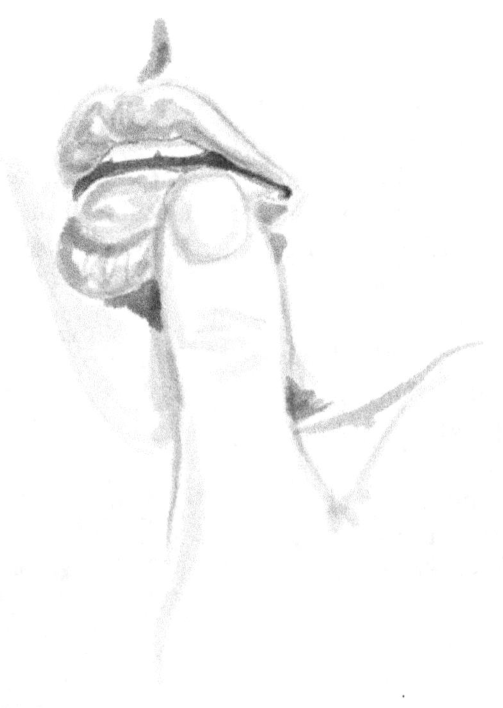

Risk It All

Like stepping into quicksand, your all-consuming grip (fingers interlaced, palms kissing, desires fused) causes a flare-up of possessiveness. I relish watching your impulse to risk it all seize you the moment your fingers connect with my skin. The taste of my moans in your mouth unearths an oceanic yearning for all the possibilities. I too will risk it all for this unparalleled feeling of carefree that we envelop each other with.

Craving

Unclothed was not naked enough for the way our souls **craved** each other.

Light

Please, keep writing and rhyming.
You breathe life into my mornings, noons, and
nights.
Sadly, life has conspired against us with its poor
timing,
and I still don't understand how one person can
radiate so much light.

82

LIVE, FULLY

Sasha Nudél

84

Anew

If I had a chance to create the world anew,
what would I do?
I would start with myself.
I would dive into every connection
with sheer, unbridled expression,
and plenitude of affection
for myself.
I promise,
I would always be tenderly honest
with myself.
I would know early on that
perfection is paralyzing,
and the beauty in recognizing
that flaws can be strikingly mesmerizing
would take so much pressure
off of myself.
In my world, gratitude would be the currency
I would use to acquire my wealth
of compassion and kindness
for others and, most importantly,
for myself.
And for every mistake made,
I would admire the courage in each fall.
For without them, I would be nowhere at all.
And courageously, I would applaud
myself.

Strong

Nothing makes you stronger than your
vulnerability.

Rejections

We posture ourselves away from rejections
only to realize,
they are simply adjustments
that bring about proper
body, mind and soul alignment.

Gem

I am a precious gem with black onyx desires in a
crystal-clear society.

This Moment

Nothing but this moment belongs to me.
Not the clothes I wear or the pain I bare.
Not the gems I own, not the evil phone.
I don't own my future.
I exist in the here and now,
and this chaos of not knowing makes living
effortless, somehow.
I don't belong to my past, my mistakes, my haters
and their pitiful gossip,
and I don't care to keep a perfectly organized
closet.
I don't need religion to find the meaning of life.
I don't seek the truth.
I just want you and I to enjoy our youth.
The youth that lasts from the very beginning to
the very end.
We don't age. We simply move closer to a graceful
descend.

Heart To Heart

If I said you had a beautiful heart,
would you hold it against me?
Would you hold it against mine?

Loneliness

People speak of loneliness,
a feeling so unfamiliar to me.
How can I feel lonely when every day
the sky embraces me,
the earth caresses my feet,
the sun plants warm tender kisses on my forehead,
the air fills my lungs with inspiration,
the ocean dedicates poems to me.

No Ordinary

Nostalgia is in my DNA makeup.
Melancholy runs in my bloodstream.
And I can't help but poeticize
even the ordinary into a beautiful dream.

Defying Time

If you were to ask me
what me and Bukowski had in common:
It must be the trauma
of knowing how fragile and short,
off and on, full of hurt
this life is.
But it is with absolute clarity,
an open mind and a healthy dose of vulgarity,
both Bukowski and I
could assure and assert through a perfect rhyme,
that to overlove
is to defy time.

Reminder

Time is palpable. It pulsates inside me like a vital organ. A simultaneously fragile and omnipotent clicking reminder to stare at the sunset a little longer, to indulge in the company of my favorite people a little deeper, to luxuriate in the togetherness with a lover more vulnerably, to plunge into this journey of life headlong. Tick. Tock.

Take It From A Poet

I think everything in life is poetry. Take it from a multi-passionate self-expressionist who marvels at the swirl in the foam of a morning matcha. Take it from a hopeless romantic who gets lost in a reverie at the thought of a lover's touch. Take it from a hopeful realist who romanticizes **death,** for there is no better reminder to indulge in the here and now. Take it from an impractical dreamer who finds utopia in every profound connection. Take it from a poet.

Poetry

Poetry is the smoothest and safest drug you can
consume.

Courage

I have a life-long muse, and she is wild and
courageous.
She teaches me to be open-minded, empathetic
and creatively outrageous.
She pushes me to look at the world from another
person's perspective,
humbles me and reminds me to be self-reflective.
She once inspired me to dismantle
society's unreasonably imposed beliefs
when I was feeling discouraged,
and that was when I learned that curiosity begets
courage.
Curiosity is my muse's name and her unapologetic
audacity
is what I aspire to exemplify.
And the most prized lesson she ever taught me:
for those without courage, magic is hard to come
by.

Motto

Less entitled. More enlightened.

98

Abundance

Fall.
Fall hard.
Fall boldly.
Fall shamelessly.
Fall harder than the guard you are putting up.
Fall to crack yourself open and show the
abundance of love you carry inside.
Because you do.
We all do.
Fall.

Ego Mania

Do not let a *rare* incident of a once-in-a-lifetime connection get ruined by a *common* mania of the ego.

Birth Day

Another revolution around the sun.
Someone told me they wished they could see the
world through my eyes.
And when I asked 'why,'
they told me they have never felt a connection to
life more potent
after I insisted they searched for heaven in every
dull moment.
After all, your holy abode is in the here and now,
in all the fragments and glimpses,
in all the hits and misses,
in all the smiles, frown lines, and freckles,
in every sky that is star-speckled.
Even the empty hellos and painful goodbyes
are simply the moments to be poeticized.
I made someone wish they could see the world
through my eyes.
The wish I made every time I have blown out a
birthday candle
has finally actualized.

Vulnerability

She was unabashed and proud of the furor her vulnerability provoked.

Exhausted

Do not be complacent.
Dance, kiss, dare, jump over a fire.
The only time you are allowed to feel tired
is when you have exhausted
all of your creativity, vigor,
passion, love, and desire.

Meaningful

Life is like a poem.
It does not have to be long to be meaningful.

Make Art

I hope you make some art this coming year.
Of love, of empathy,
of kindness, of kissing,
of touching, of dreaming,
of dancing, of self-care, of giving.
Some art of courage for an unforgettable story.
Now repeat your new mantra:
'No guts, no glory.'

Creativity

Always choose creativity over certainty.

106

Life

Life.
I am not in it just for a voyeur's delight.
This hearty appetite
is meant to taste every corner of every emotion,
to dive deep in a bottomless ocean,
to partake in a grand love story
of which I am the prime suspect,
to experience love as scary as an unidentified
flying object.
I am in it to create a rapid-fire montage
of all the striking moments,
but commit only the best ones to memory:
egos breaking, souls colliding, getting lost in
perpetual reverie.

Chaos

Chaos makes the poet.

Rebellion

Life smiles at me like she is privy to something
that I am not.
"What are you thinking?" I ask.
She advises me to stop playing it safe and I eagerly
oblige. I erase the line between mad and
courageous, for they mean the same thing, and
proceed to engage in the ultimate act of poetic
rebellion: living my life to the fullest.

Remarkable Moments

Just making sure the old lady
with memories of a time gone by
will have some remarkable moments
to reminisce about before the final goodbye.

Delicate Planet

Today the storm has given the earth a much
needed bath.
The cleaning took place in the immediate
aftermath
of a major disaster.
The earth was being showered with love, light and
laughter,
and then unexpectedly set on fire,
from the lowest, deepest layer and all the way to
the highest.
Now the earth wears a newly-acquired burn scar.
Seen from both near and far,
the intricacy of her blueprint
of all the wounds she carries within.
Unlike all other celestial bodies,
she is the only one to host life in the Universe.
Both a blessing for her and a curse.
And although she is tougher than granite,
remember, she still is just a delicate planet.

Nudists

I am setting off on a daring adventure to discover
my own depths.
An escape from a landlocked life to explore the
shores occupied with the like-minded:
soul nudists with bare hearts.

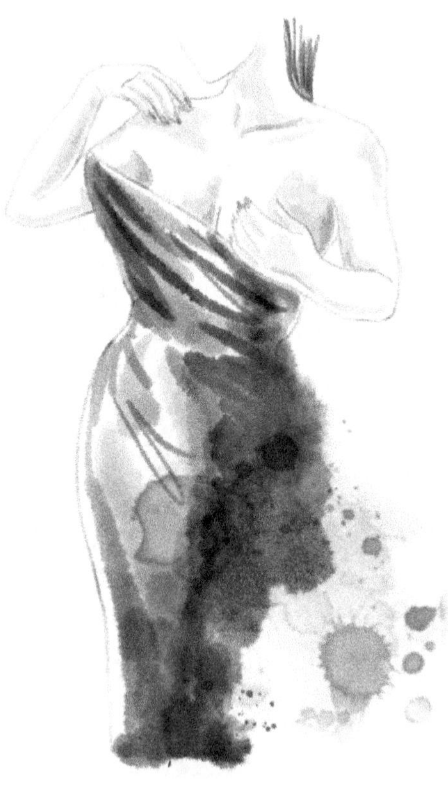

Blink

I love it when the sky makes me feel insignificant.
The daily changes in its color are emblematic of
how temperamental life is. All we have to do is
accept the mood swings. How will you know to
appreciate the blueness never
having had blackness to
compare it to?
Blink, darkness. Blink,
brightness.
Blink, chaos. Blink,
blank slate.
Blink, worries. Blink,
peace.
Blink, the vast
nothingness of every
day begging
to be made
into
something
glorious.

Fall

My favorite season is the Fall of the ego.

114

Love Unites

Whether your wine is red or white,
aged or young.
Whether you agree or fight,
speak your mind or hold your tongue.
Whether you pray or simply hope,
idolize the left or the right.
Whether you are rich or broke,
life is not plainly black and white.
Whether you are hard-hearted or tender,
no matter where you find your delight.
In war and in peace, just remember,
love unites.

Heavy Artillery

In a time of internal war,
when your heart is bursting at the seams with
misery,
it is a poet's sense of hope
that is the real heavy artillery.

Twinkle

Strive to waste as little time as possible.
For that, end all thoughts of the improbable
and don't let things that are out of your control
swallow you whole.
Pride yourself on artfully befriending **Fear**.
A message here to ring clear
is that you are to drive inspiration
from both scary and painful but beautifully
transformational,
for pain is always purposeful, educational.
Love yourself relentlessly and without
comparison.
Your flaws are your attributes, not
embarrassments.
Lean into the things that make you come alive.
It truly is that simple.
Every single soul deserves to twinkle.

Now

The word 'now' is so invigorating. The urgency in it is like a razor-sharp gust of wind rushing me to live in the moment. The word 'now' is so hypnotic. It summons me to give wings to my imagination. The word 'now' is so provocative. It demands I feel and make others feel.

Not Afraid To Die

When you know the fabric of time is thin.
When you realize the root of *sin*cere is sin.
When you fail to find the good in *good*bye.
When you learn you are being fed a lie.
When the heartbreak makes your ribs crackle.
When saving broken glass is fighting a losing
battle.
When the pit in your stomach is no longer
butterfly flutter.
When your daydreams are now just hurtful mind
clutter.
When pain camouflages itself in a smile,
I start to understand why.
Why so many people are not afraid to die.

(Be)longing

I feel unsettled in and about my life, like it doesn't belong to me, like I don't belong to it. And it's the gnawing knowing in my chest that gives me hope that somewhere in a parallel universe, I'm living the life that I belong to.

De-armor

I willingly lend my being to the thrall of pain,
melancholy and nostalgia, because I am convinced
that the only way to achieve emotional sturdiness
is by making space for vulnerability in your life.
What used to be a rigid armor over my chest is
now a delicate blouse offering a tender embrace.
Turns out, the armor I was wearing all my life was
just useless scrap metal. Had I not realized sooner,
the armor could have hindered my life force from
flowing freely through my body, could have
obstructed my potential, could have stalled my
creativity. The porous fabric of my new blouse
allows me to breathe fully, openly, and frees me
from the counterproductive physical and
emotional blockages.
My openness is my protection.

Muse

Muse: one's deepest, heaviest, most chest-
constricting sigh of despair & relief.

Exciting

It was exciting,
absolutely.
Feeling nature so acutely.
Running a splinter into my finger
while climbing the tree on a sidewalk.
Jumping through puddles and the only struggle
was running out of street chalk.

Hiding and seeking with the jolly sun peeping
over our freckled ears.
Going the distance to enjoy our existence.
We were onto something as kids!

Everything felt fantastically terrifying.
No option of quitting,
we would simply keep trying
in every adventure we leapt at.
Authentic, joyous, observant, brilliant,
unfiltered, rebellious, daring, resilient.
Why do grownups forget that?

Beyond

Wandering past the horizon.
Sensing beyond the deepest feeling.
Imagining beyond the end of the world.
Creating beyond certainty.

Your Heart Is a Fist

At the risk of sounding trite,
allow me to remind
that your heart's primary function is to contract.
In fact,
after contraction it will expand,
and since you are in command
of your reactions to various turns of events,
planned and unplanned,
your heart is both spacious and grand
to acknowledge, sit with, and process
all that you feel.
Be it love too damn surreal,
profound intimacy, nagging heartache,
or inexplicable bliss.
Your heart is a mighty fist!
The one that will punch against what doesn't seem
right.
And other times, clenched snug and tight,
it will embrace and hold onto
whatever makes the lighthearted feel light.

Let Them Know

For the love of poetry, please, do not hoard your feelings. Do you really want a lifetime to go by without letting them know how they made you feel?

Inspiration

I am overcome with tender pity and sadness
for that girl right across my table.
While I'm enjoying the most decadent breakfast,
her empty eyes are glued to her phone,
aimlessly scrolling through content of the author
unknown.
I wish she had known
she had just missed the sunrays dancing
across her toast,
and her artfully served coffee roasts
are now tasteless and cold.
Just like her world.
My world.
Our world.
The one that commodified our likes and dislikes,
and things that were viewed as unique are now
standardized.
Knowledge, skill, culture, experience are now all
dispensable.
What a shame. What a spectacle.
We ought to *re*learn the rules of in-person
conversation.
We ought to *un*learn this addiction to digital
stimulation.
Technology often feeds us with vain promises and
illusory treats.
Oh how unkempt our internal landscape must be.
Let's tidy it up by weeding out the need for
computerized validation,
for scrolling and clicking is certainly not how you
nurture inspiration.

More

She just wanted to leave them with a little more than what they had when they first met her. More feelings, more purpose, more poetry. Silken words and tender moments to last a lifetime.

Playful Sentimentality

Hardheadedness failed me. It will fail you too. It will depreciate the value of your heart. Instead, find that bud of sentimentality inside your chest and allow it to open up into a bloom. Get lost in the unleashed moments of life. Unstructured, free flowing. Grant free rein to your monumental imagination. Be playful. Play ignites creativity. Creativity generates joy. The world desperately needs a widespread flowering of playful sentimentality.

Wild

A flower grows vigorously in the wild.

130

Fulfilling

To stay true to yourself in brazen defiance of societal norms is to live a fulfilling life. Tragically, most are too buttoned-up to understand.

Curiosity

A wildly inappropriate curiosity is a stepping stone
to enlightenment.

Fail

Failures were invented so that you could find your purpose.

Traveling Poem

I am relishing world's twists, turns and zigzags
as a proud owner of hundreds of jet lags.
Breaking stilettos on European cobblestones,
exploring areas bougainvillea is native to,
carelessly devouring pizza in Naples,
introducing my dresses to wine stains,
getting my ankles covered in puddles
during the London rain.
I am collecting adventures so surreal
into a technicolor memory reel.
I am unlocking time's merciless grip
with unplanned trips- the antidote to stagnation.
Traveling is what gives wings to my imagination.

Love Yourself

But most importantly, fall in love with yourself, so you will never know what unrequited love feels like.

Happily Ever After

I don't have a dream destination, rather a dream
path.
My life's aftermath
isn't a worry,
even when I am recklessly tiptoeing
on the thin line between rational and impulsive,
calm and explosive,
when I choose to live life in big doses,
when I don't live by default, rather on purpose.
When I don't seek truths in others,
for they are not found in friends or lovers,
but in your gut, the world's eighth wonder.
On my dream path,
I don't put my curiosity to rest. I take chances.
I enjoy conversations with no real answers.
To find magic in the tingling of your fingertips,
through the tears and the laughter,
is my kind of *happily ever after.*

Table Of Contents

LOVE, ALWAYS

LIVE, FULLY

ACKNOWLEDGEMENTS

I would like to express my deepest gratitude to the readers of my poetry. Your presence and engagement with my words have been truly invaluable. Thank you for taking the time to delve into the world I've created with my poems, for allowing my words to resonate within your own experiences, thoughts, and emotions. Your willingness to embark on this poetic journey with me is both humbling and inspiring. Your support has been a constant source of motivation.

To my husband and my parents, thank you for your constant understanding and patience as I explored the depths of my imagination. Your unwavering support and belief in my talent have given me the courage to pursue my passion for poetry.

To my best friend, thank you for being my sounding board, for listening to my musings and offering constructive feedback. Your encouragement and belief in my abilities have fueled my creativity and pushed me to reach new heights. Your friendship has been an endless source of inspiration and profound joy.

Thank you to the incredible publishing team of Pen2Publish for their expertise in navigating the publishing world. My sincere appreciation goes to Allie Michelle for her insightful feedback, suggestions and guidance, Jordyn Denning for her invaluable editing contributions in shaping and refining this book, Anfisa Kuzmina for the beautiful cover and interior design that brought my book to life.

To my muses, thank you for breathing life into the verses that have poured from my heart onto these pages.

With profound gratitude,

Sasha

ABOUT THE AUTHOR

Sasha Nudél, a Ukraine-born poet, speech-language pathologist and certified fitness trainer, is a multifaceted individual driven by a passion for diverse pursuits. Sasha's evocative musings and poems delve into the depths of love, sensuality, the lust for life, and the profound nature of human connection. With a gift for crafting soul-stirring words, she takes readers on a transformative journey through the realms of emotion and desire.-Through her distinctive voice and profound understanding of the human condition, she captures the essence of passion and longing, weaving together verses that resonate deeply. Her writings serve as a powerful reminder of the beauty and connection found in the exploration of human intimacy.

Currently residing in the vibrant city of Brooklyn, NY, Sasha continues to share her captivating verses with a growing audience. For an immersive experience into her world, follow Sasha's poetic journey on Instagram @sashanudel.

146